Owen & The Old Willow Tree Owl

Owen & The Old Willow Tree Owl

A FIRST CHAPTER BOOK FOR KIDS

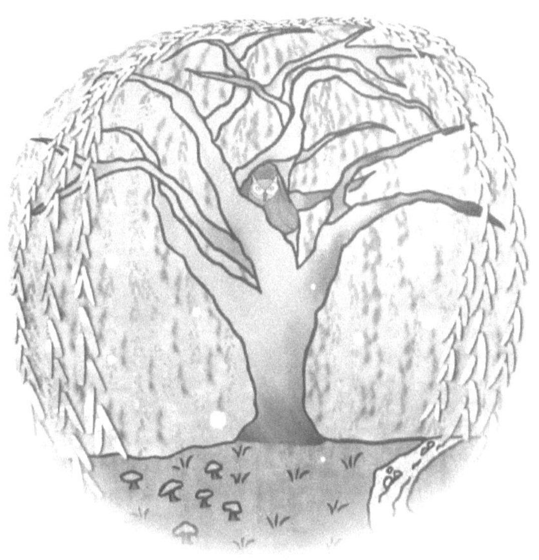

Written & Illustrated by

CHRISTY BRUNKEN

For my 4 beautiful, wonderful, super inspiring children. Anything good I do is all because of you.

ISBN: 9798585108556

Download **FREE** activities, educational printables, and extra bookmarks for this book at:

pk1homeschoolfun.com/owen

Cut out this bookmark

and Owen will fly with you as you read this book!

Cut the thick dotted lines on Owen's wings and he'll keep your spot for you!

Table of Contents

CHAPTER ONE

Chip had never seen a raspberry bush come alive before.

It was shaking and grunting. It looked like it was about to grow legs and stomp around the forest.

He imagined raspberries flying everywhere.

He would have been afraid to get any closer. But Chip was the fastest squirrel around. He zipped up close enough to get a better look. He stayed

back far enough away to run – just in
case the raspberry bush tried anything
funny.

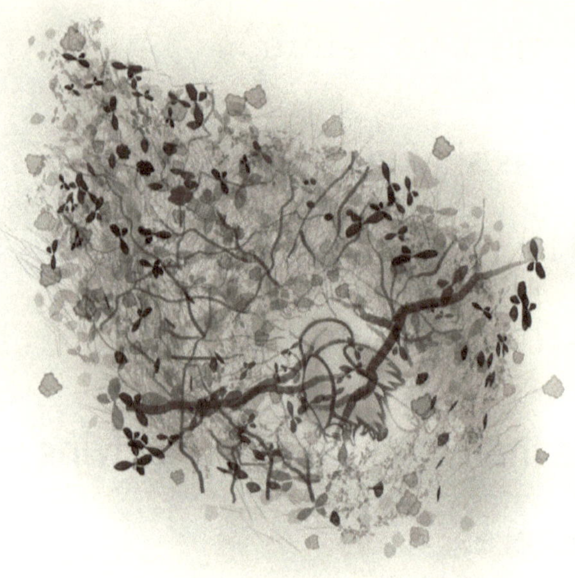

Now Chip could see a mess of brown
feathers flapping about in the stickers of
the bush. Ripe red raspberries thrashed
here and there.

Chip's best friend Owen wiggled backwards out of the bramble.

Owen turned to face him. Chip could see something large and stick-like in his beak.

Owen dropped the object on the ground. He took some big puffs of air. He looked like the happiest little owl that Chip had ever seen.

"Hi, Chip! Look what I found!" Owen shouted.

Owen was so excited that his feet

were bopping about. His wings flapped up and down as he danced.

The two best friends looked down at the strange sticks.

There were two flat pieces of wood.

One crossed through the other. They had strange red markings and one had a red tip.

Neither of them knew what it was. Finding something new in the forest was very exciting!

"What is it?" Chip asked.

"I don't know, but it sure is interesting!" Owen answered. "Maybe we should take it to Sam!"

If anyone could figure out what it was, it would be Sam, their fox friend.

Owen picked up the object in his

beak. It was twice his size. It was terribly difficult to both walk *and* see at the same time.

Owen had only just learned how to fly. He knew his wings were not strong enough to carry both him and the fancy sticks. So Owen walked with Chip towards the fox den where Sam lived.

He hobbled along carrying the awkward sticks. He walked a little slanted, using mostly one eye to see where he was going.

Chip bounded alongside him,

making all sorts of guesses about what the two flat wooden sticks were.

"Maybe they're some kind of instrument," Chip chattered away, "or a funny rake, or a hairbrush for a giraffe!"

The two friends walked on a skinny log to cross a creek.

Some tiny forest finches flew in loopy circles above them. The small birds tweeted about Owen's new find. They swooped down low to get a better look. Then they flew up fast into the treetops.

"What did you find, what did you

find?" The finches chirped. They fluttered from branch to branch above them.

"We're not sure," called Chip.

"Owen found it in the raspberry bushes."

The finches offered some wild and silly guesses about what the sticks were. Then they flew away as quickly as they had appeared.

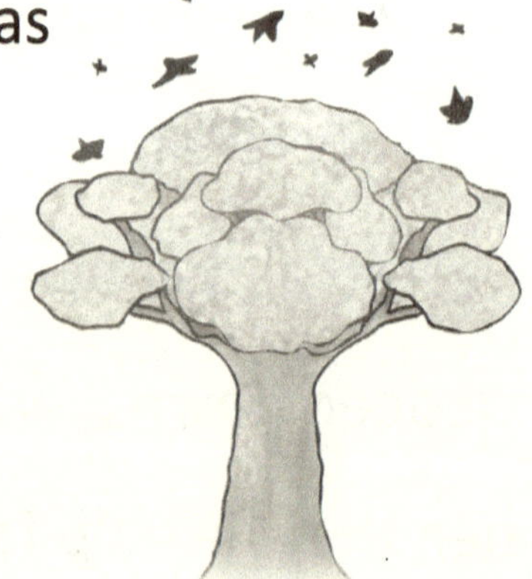

CHAPTER TWO

When they reached the fox den, Owen whistled a few special notes. A nose poked out of a hole in a giant fallen log.

Suddenly a flash of orange fur whizzed about them. Sam knocked Owen down with her happy hello.

"Hiya, Owen! Good morning, Chip!" The young fox jumped about as she greeted her friends.

"Hey, Sam! How are ya?" Chip asked

her.

Sam wrinkled her nose. She shook her head a little.

"It's been a weird day," she said.

"There were hundreds of finches swirling in the sky. They warned me that some bears with big sticks were coming our way, but I didn't believe them.

"If any bears do show up, I'll fight them off. You just wait and see!"

Sam ran

around fast in small circles. Then she jumped up and shook her white-tipped paws in the air.

"Um, I don't think that story is quite right," Owen said, giggling.

"Chip and I are the ones with the special sticks. I found them in the raspberry bush. But they're not big, and we're not bears!"

"Well, those finches were chattering away really fast," Sam explained. "It was tough to get the whole story from them.

"I may have made some of that up."

Sam smiled and said she was sorry for fibbing.

"So are these the sticks you found?" Sam asked.

She snatched the sticks from Owen and looked them over. She pulled one stick out of the other one. Then she put it back into its slot.

"Do you know what it is?" Chip asked Sam, his eyes wide with curiosity.

"You were smart to come to me, guys." Sam said. "I know *exactly* what this is!"

Owen felt pretty proud of himself for thinking to take the sticks to Sam.

Sam was the smartest fox he'd ever met. You had to be careful with her stories, though. She always had trouble telling only the facts. Sometimes she added extra bits that weren't quite true.

For the most part, the little fox really did know a lot about most things.

"This-" Sam cleared her throat, "- is a gliding sword!"

Owen and Chip gasped. It was even better than they had imagined.

CHAPTER THREE

"A gliding sword?" The two friends asked at the same time.

"Yes!" Sam exclaimed. "You put it together like this."

Sam fixed the sticks so they were straight.

"Then, you...throw it at your enemy!"

Sam threw the glider into the air, red tip first. It glided smoothly up, up, and up.

Then it glided down and took a nose dive. It crashed into a gopher hole.

"Whoa!" Owen yelled. "Did you see that, Chip?"

Chip was already at the gopher hole and picked up the glider.

"It doesn't seem to hit what you aim at," Chip observed. "And it doesn't feel sharp."

"It doesn't look scary," Owen added, "or dangerous. I don't think it's a sword."

Sam answered quickly. "Well, maybe this is more like a toy and not a weapon. I still think you could nail a naughty toad with it if you had to!"

Chip stood on his two back paws. He threw the glider just as Sam had done. It flew through the air.

This time it landed gently on a patch of grass by Sam's den.

The three friends played with the gliding sticks for awhile. Chip dragged it high up a tree. He threw it from the tree top to see how far it would fly.

It went so far that they all had to vote on who would go get it.

Both Owen and Sam picked Chip because he was the fastest of them all.

Then Sam thought Owen should race the glider.

Owen got ready to race. He wiggled his tail feathers. He fixed his gaze on the old willow tree.

Even though he was new at flying, he was sure he could beat a couple of sticks.

"On your mark, get set, GO!" Sam yelled.

She threw the glider as hard and as

fast as she could. It sailed through the air.

Owen took off in a cloud of dust. He flapped his small wings as hard as he could.

Up and up he went. He caught up to the glider. He nudged ahead of it a little. He smiled as he pumped his wings.

Of course he was winning.

Just then a gush of wind blew and pushed the glider along with it.

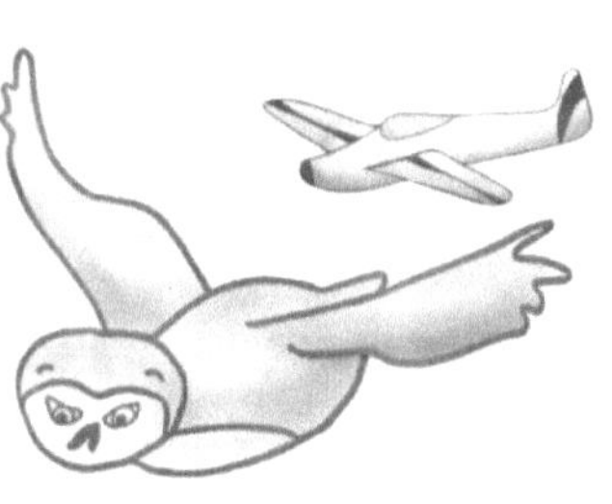

The glider was lighter than Owen.

That made it faster in the wind.

The wind swiftly carried the glider into the branches of the old willow tree.

By the time Owen reached the willow tree, he was completely out of breath. He landed and took a moment to rest.

Sam and Chip caught up to him.

"Wow! I can't believe the glider won," Chip said.

Owen hung his head a little.

"It's ok, Owen," Sam said. "I saw

that gust of wind pick up the glider in a flurry of leaves. That was an unfair race."

Owen looked around a little. "Where's the glider?" The three friends looked all around the willow tree but did not see it.

Sam was the first to say the bad news.

"Guys," she said slowly, "I think the glider is *inside* the willow tree's canopy."

The old willow tree was a very big and old weeping willow. Its long branches draped all the way down to the ground.

They were so thick that you couldn't see even a little bit through them.

The darkness inside the willow tree's canopy was scary enough. Even scarier, though, was the Old Willow Tree Owl who lived inside.

The three friends had to take another vote.

Chip was fast, but Owen could fly. Sam was smart and clever.

But who was brave enough to peek into the willow tree to look for the glider?

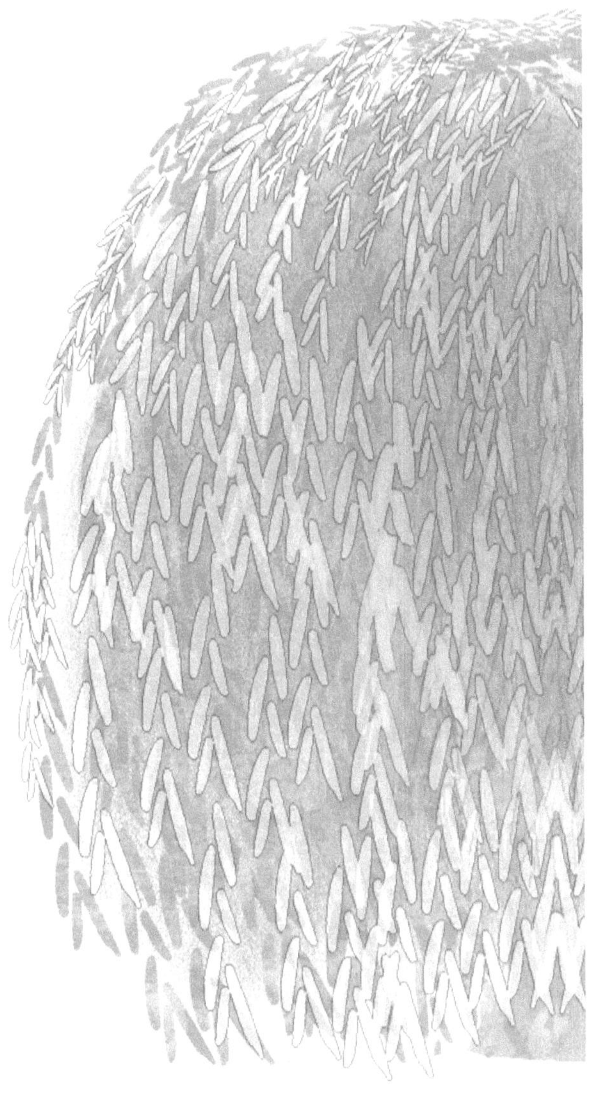

CHAPTER FOUR

"I heard the Old Willow Tree Owl eats squirrels for snacks," Chip said, shaking.

"I heard the Old Willow Tree Owl is the wisest animal in the forest. I could never outsmart him if he caught me," Sam said.

"My mom told me to never go into the old willow tree, but she never said why. I don't dare disobey my mom," Owen said firmly.

The three friends stood there looking sad for a moment.

"I had better get home," Chip said. "I need to do my morning chores."

Owen realized Chip was right. The sun was rising higher in the sky and he was feeling sleepy. Little owls sleep during the day and shouldn't be out long past sunrise.

Sam tried to cheer them up. "Maybe tomorrow we'll find something else in the raspberry bushes!"

Owen said goodbye to Chip and

Sam. He flew to his oak tree at the edge of the forest. He couldn't wait to get to his cozy hollow. He wanted to tell his mom all about finding the glider.

Maybe he would skip the part about losing it in the old willow tree.

Owen ducked his head into the hollow and saw his mom lying in bed. His dad was perched next to her with a sad look on his face.

"Hello, Owen." His dad said. He turned his head around to see his son.

"What happened to Mom?" Owen asked.

Owen's dad hopped down from his mom's bedside. His big strong wings stretched out and brought Owen near.

"Owen, your mom is very sick," his dad explained.

Owen had never seen his dad so sad before. Owen took a closer look at his mom. She looked sweet and kind like always. She didn't look sick to him.

"Is she going to be ok?" Owen asked.

"I don't know," Owen's dad replied.

"She needs a special tea made from a goldenseal flower. The doctor doesn't have any. No one has seen that flower in this forest for many years."

Owen looked at his dad and then at his mom. First he lost his special glider and now his mom was sick. He had been so happy earlier to find the new toy.

Now he felt it was the saddest night he'd ever had.

"Get to sleep, son," Owen's dad told him. "We'll know more in the evening."

Owen settled into his soft nest. Tears welled up in his eyes. He wiped them with his shoulder feathers. He shut his eyes and went to sleep.

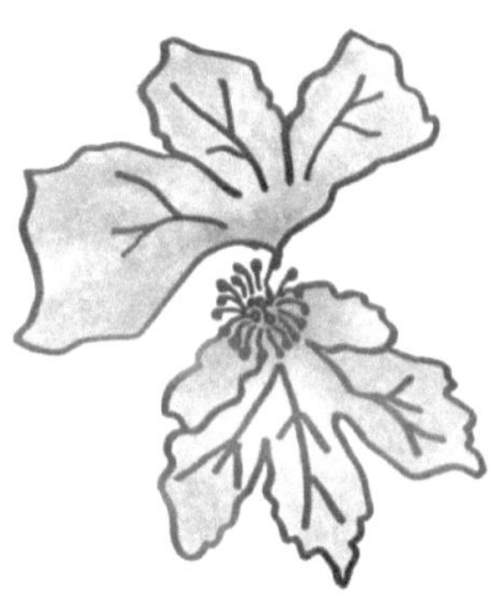

That night he dreamed of goldenseal flowers. They danced in the moonlight and called out his name. And then he dreamed of the Old Willow Tree Owl –

the wisest animal in the forest.

And when he woke up the next night

he knew exactly what to do.

CHAPTER FIVE

The very moment the sun started to go lower in the sky, Owen was awake. His mom and dad were still sleeping. He quietly slipped out of his nest and hopped out of his hollow.

Owen flew straight to that old willow tree. He landed on the ground where its branches dangled in the dirt.

He looked the tree up and down. He tried to feel brave.

Owen hopped a few steps towards

the branches. The leaves of the willow tree were golden in the light of the sunset.

Owen squirmed through the branches. The moment he had pushed through them all, everything went dark.

It was like he was inside a giant dome. The willow tree branches hung around him like walls. They blocked out all the light from the outside.

Owen's eyes could see better in the dark. He now clearly saw everything around him.

Wavy capped mushrooms grew all

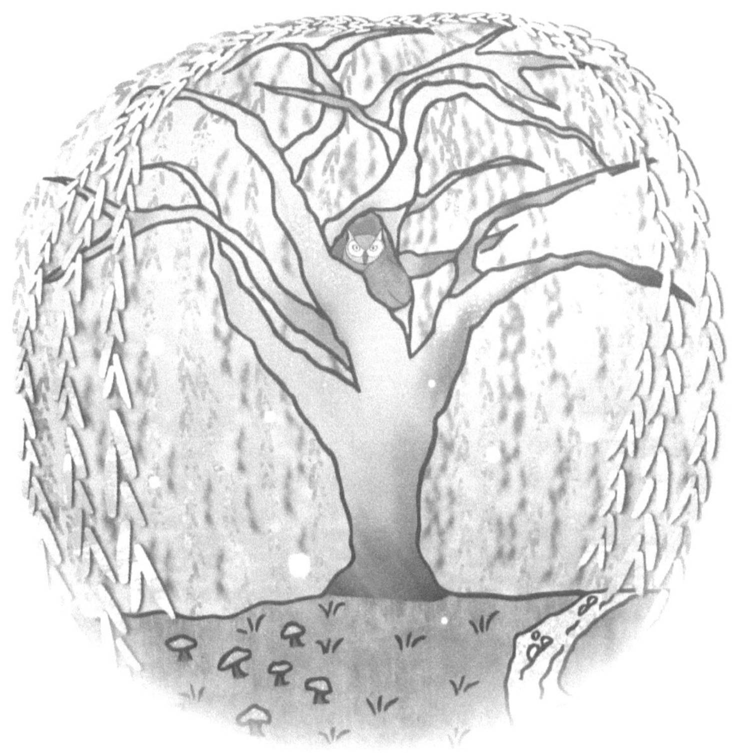

along the ground. A very tiny stream

flowed nearby. Little blinking lights from

fireflies sparkled in the darkness.

Owen walked towards the willow tree's trunk. Suddenly, something snapped beneath his foot. A net closed up around him and whisked him up, up, up to the top of the tree.

He flapped his wings wildly. He tried to figure out which way was up and which way was down. Finally, he held still and dangled for a moment.

"Who...?" A slow, raspy call came

from the tree.

"Who....is....in...my...tree...?" The voice asked.

Owen tried to speak. Only a little squeak came out. He coughed a little. Then spoke up in the bravest voice he could make.

"Please get me out of this net!" He pleaded.

"You...," the voice responded, "look like a very lost little owl."

The voice spoke slowly. Owen thought he heard a little chuckle.

The net swung a little. It opened onto a large thick branch. Owen spilled out of the net. His feet landed flat on the branch. He stood up.

The Old Willow Tree Owl stood there in front of him. His eyes were large and yellow. His brow made a giant "V" at the top of his face.

Owen couldn't tell if the old owl was angry or amused.

"I am sorry about my trap," the owl said. "I find the nets to be the most clever way to catch mice.

"But you," the owl stooped down and took a closer look at Owen, "are NOT a mouse!"

"No, I am not!" Owen answered him.

"In that case, allow me to introduce myself."

The Old Willow Tree Owl gave a little bow. "My name is Victor and this is my willow tree."

"Hello, Victor," Owen said politely. "I'm Owen. My family lives in the old oak tree just past the edge of the forest."

"Ah, yes," said Victor, picturing it in his mind. "I know the tree and I know of your parents."

"You do?" Owen asked, surprised.

"Why, yes," Victor chuckled. "I know about nearly every creature in these woods. How are your mom and dad?"

Owen looked down at his feet. He thought about his sweet mom. He thought about how sick she was. He tried not to cry.

"My mom is very sick. In fact, that's why I'm here," Owen answered him.

"I am sorry to hear that your mom is sick," Victor replied. He flew to a more comfortable branch nearby. "However, I am thankful to have a visitor. Now come and tell me how I can help."

Owen flew over to the branch Victor had perched on. He told him how his mom needed a tea made from a goldenseal flower. He told him that the doctor did not have any. No one knew where to find them.

Victor was silent for awhile. He tilted his head to the left. He tilted it to the right. His tummy feathers puffed up a little. His eyes widened.

"The doctor is correct," Victor spoke slowly. "The goldenseal flower is very difficult to find. But not impossible." He winked at Owen.

Owen jumped up. "I knew it!" He shouted. "I knew you would know where to find them!"

"Now, now," Victor tried to calm him down. "There were always goldenseal flowers near the watering hole. I have not heard if they are still there. But I remember them well enough."

Owen was thrilled at this news. He could hardly sit still.

"Please, can you tell me where the watering hole is? I have never heard of it."

"It is very far from here. I do not think you can make the journey alone," Victor warned him. "You'll need to send your dad."

"Oh, no." Owen stubbornly disagreed. "There isn't time! I need to get the flower tonight! Won't you take me there?"

Victor shuddered. He jumped off his branch and flew around the willow tree trunk twice.

He disappeared into his hollow.

CHAPTER SIX

Owen looked around, stunned. He flew over to Victor's hollow and looked inside.

"What's wrong?" He asked. "Won't you take me?"

Victor poked his beak out of the hollow. Owen jumped back.

"I am very sorry for your mom, but I cannot take you."

"But, why not?" Owen whined a little.

Victor hobbled out of his hole a few steps. He sighed.

"I have not left this willow tree in ten years. I have not left it since the great fire."

Now Victor looked even sadder than Owen.

The Old Willow Tree Owl told Owen that he had lost his whole family in that fire. He himself had barely escaped.

After the fire he found this great willow tree. Its thick branches and dark canopy made him feel safe.

He decided to make it his home and never, ever leave.

"So you've been alone for ten years?" Owen asked, concerned. He couldn't imagine not having a family or friends.

"Oh, the finches come by every sunset when I wake up. They tell me all about what's happening in the forest. But I admit, I have been a little lonely lately."

Victor looked at the thick branches of the willow tree. For a few moments he wondered what it would be like to fly across the night sky.

"Well, you're not alone anymore. I'm your friend and I will come visit you every day," Owen said.

Victor closed his eyes and took a deep breath. Then he opened them and looked kindly at Owen.

"You are a very nice little owl, Owen.

"I know what the forest animals say about me. It's easy for them to make up scary stories about someone they've never met. It took a lot of courage for you to come here."

Victor stood up straight. He stretched his wings out and his neck up high. Then he settled his feathers.

"If you can be so brave," Victor paused a moment, "so can I.

"Let's go find those goldenseal flowers, little owl!"

CHAPTER SEVEN

Owen flew up and plopped onto Victor's back. He ducked his head down. He held on tight with his talons.

"Ready, little owl?" Victor asked. He sounded nervous, but excited too.

"Let's go, Willow Tree Owl!" Owen shouted.

Victor flew towards the willow tree branches. He nudged into them and out the other side. A fresh breeze brought old familiar smells of the night.

Victor's giant wings pushed the two owls higher into the sky. They soared above the treetops. The moonlight shone onto the forest below them.

Owen could see his oak tree to the left. The forest went on to the right as far as he could see.

The little owl had never traveled so far from home. Hours went by in flight.

Owen saw a clearing in the trees. Muddy water sparkled in a pool below them. It was the watering hole.

Victor swooped down for a closer look. There on the muddy banks of the watering hole was a mess of goldenseal leaves.

The flowers had been trampled on

by the many waterhole visitors. Victor spotted one perfect goldenseal flower left in the middle of the patch.

Before he could snatch up the flower, a family of bobcats came walking towards the watering hole.

The two owls flew away to a nearby pine tree.

"Did you see any flowers?" Owen asked, hopeful.

"The goldenseal patch has been trampled by all the animals that come here. I saw just one perfect flower in the patch," Victor explained.

"But those bobcats mean trouble for us." Victor looked very worried.

"I am an old owl," Victor told Owen. "The bobcats will overtake me if I go down there. And you are too small. They would love to have you as a snack!"

Victor paused, trying to figure out what to do.

"We need a distraction!" Owen said, sure of himself. "I'll get the bobcats to go to those trees over there. Then, you swoop down and get the flower!"

"No, Owen," Victor said sternly. "It's much too dangerous."

Owen was sad. He thought of his mom. He would do anything to help her.

Before Victor could stop him, Owen flew off to distract the bobcats.

Owen was a small owl, but tonight he flew faster than he ever had.

When he reached the trees, Owen chirped a distress call.

The bobcats knew that sound. It meant a small owl was in trouble. It meant there was an easy snack nearby.

One of the bobcats was bigger than the rest. He was their leader. He led all the bobcats to the tree branch where Owen was chirping.

The bobcats stalked up the tree. The

leader locked his eyes on Owen and licked his lips!

Victor was worried about Owen, but now there wer no bobcats at the watering hole. Victor looked down at that last goldenseal flower below.

Now was his chance.

He swooped down quickly and landed in the goldenseal patch. He snatched the flower in his beak. He opened his wings to fly off. He could not fly. His left foot was caught in the sticky mud!

Owen saw Victor in the mud. It was time to fly off and help his friend!

Owen flapped his wings quickly. They barely lifted him up off the branch. His poor wings were tired out from all that fast flying.

Owen looked at the lead bobcat. In a few moments he could leap and catch Owen in his teeth.

Victor flapped and flapped with all his might. He tugged his foot as he tried to fly. He saw the bobcats get closer to Owen. He tried harder.

Owen flapped his wings as hard as he could. He spun around in circles. He lost control.

Tug, tug... TUG! Finally Victor pulled his muddy foot from the ground. His big wings carried him into the air.

Owen had never been so afraid. Suddenly Victor's back was under Owen's feet. He dug his claws into Victor's feathers and held on tight.

Victor flew him up into the sky, far away from the bobcats.

CHAPTER EIGHT

The two owls broke through the treetops. Victor flew fast and steadily towards home. In his beak he held tightly to the goldenseal flower.

They flew in silence, both happy to be safe.

Owen felt deeply thankful for Victor's help. He wondered how he could ever repay the kindness from the Old Willow Tree Owl.

Victor was thankful for Owen. All

these years he had hidden inside his willow tree. He had been so afraid of everything.

But tonight all that changed. He had met danger and survived. More importantly, he saved his friend's life. And now they were off to save Owen's mom.

Victor flew past his willow tree. He flew to the edge of the forest. He flew right to Owen's oak tree.

Owen hopped off Victor's back. Victor gave him the goldenseal flower.

"Go, Owen," Victor told him. "Go and save your mom."

Owen rushed to his dad inside.

"Owen! Where have you been?" Owen's dad sounded worried. Then he saw Victor outside their hollow. It startled him.

"I went to see the Old Willow Tree Owl," Owen answered. "His name is Victor. He took me to a goldenseal patch."

The little owl told the story as fast as he could.

"Look, Dad!" Owen shouted. He set the flower at his dad's feet. "It's a goldenseal flower!"

Owen's dad looked at the flower, then back up at Owen. He didn't speak another word. Instead, he quickly made a tea from the goldenseal flower.

He woke up Owen's mom and gave it to her to drink. She finished the tea and went back to sleep.

Owen's dad invited Victor to come inside.

"I can't thank you

enough for your help tonight," he told the Old Willow Tree Owl.

"Your son is very brave," Victor told him, "and very stubborn!"

The owls all laughed. They shared stories about the forest. Victor told Owen's dad about the great fire ten years ago. It had made him afraid of everything. It had made him alone.

"There are many empty hollows in our great oak tree," Owen's dad said. "Any one of them would make a great home for you."

Owen's eyes lit up. "We would love for you to be our neighbor! You would never be alone again!"

Victor was quiet for a few moments. He thought about leaving his willow tree. It would be hard to do. But if he moved to this great oak tree, he would not be alone.

"I will think about it. Thank you," Victor said. He looked over at Owen's mom. "I hope the goldenseal flower makes her well."

Victor got up. He said goodbye and flew home to his willow tree.

Just then, Owen's mom sat up in her nest.

"Oh, my. How long have I been asleep?" She asked.

"Mom!" Owen rushed to her side. "How are you feeling?"

"Oh, I feel wonderful!" Owen's mom answered. "Who was that owl you and Dad were talking to?"

"Oh, that was Victor, the Old Willow Tree Owl," Owen told her.

"Really?" She asked. "He didn't look as mean and scary as others say he is."

"He is very nice," Owen's dad told her. "In fact, he is the one who took Owen to find the last goldenseal flower in the forest. He saved your life."

"What a wonderful friend," she said. "We must have him over for breakfast sometime."

Owen heard Chip's chattering outside. He flew out to greet him.

"I heard your mom was sick. I came right away," he chattered on. "Is she ok?"

"Hi, Chip!" Owen greeted him. "She was very sick. But boy did you miss a night of adventure!"

Owen told Chip all about the Old Willow Tree Owl. He told them about their trip to the watering hole. He described their run-in with the bobcats.

And best of all, he told Chip how they had saved his mom with the goldenseal flower.

"I just can't believe it," Chip said.

"Which part?" Owen asked.

"Well, all of it! I thought the Old Willow Tree Owl was scary and mean. But he saved you from the bobcats and he saved your mom. Wow!"

Just then Chip and Owen were covered by a giant shadow. Victor was hovering overhead. Chip looked up at him with wide eyes.

"If you don't mind," Victor said, "I'll be moving into my new hollow now."

Owen danced around and flapped his wings. He was so happy that Victor would be their new neighbor.

"Oh," Victor added, "and I believe this belongs to you."

He pulled something out of his pack and tossed it to Owen. It was their glider!

Owen couldn't believe it. The night before had been so sad. But now he couldn't imagine any night ever being as wonderful as this one.

The sun was rising and Owen needed to get to bed. He didn't want this night to end. So Chip and Owen played with the glider for a few more minutes.

They laughed and took turns trying new tricks.

"You guys are NOT going to believe what I just heard!" Sam's voice reached Chip and Owen before she did.

"The finches would not stop tweeting about it! Last night some killer owls attacked a family of bobcats near the watering hole. Can you believe it?"

Owen and Chip looked at each other and laughed. Sam was at it again. She only had part of the story right.

"Well...?" Sam begged them to answer.

"Do you know any killer owls?"

THE END

9 798585 108556